Introduction

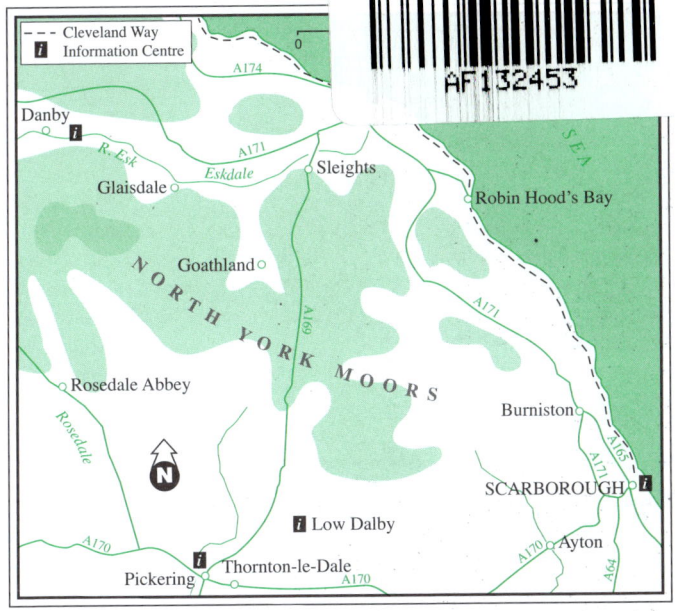

The North York Moors is an area of moorland intersected by narrow dales, butted up against the coast in the north-eastern corner of Yorkshire. The area covered measures approximately 30 miles from north to south and 40 miles from west to east. The population is low – and largely confined to villages and towns around the edge of the area. Eskdale, the largest of the dales, runs east to west across the northern part of the area; all other significant dales run approximately north to south. The area became a national park in 1952.

This series covers the North York Moors in two guides, dividing the moors into eastern and western areas. This guide covers the eastern area, including walks along the coast in the east and as far west as Danby (in the north) and Pickering (in the south).

The largest town in this area is the old port of Whitby, at the mouth of the River Esk (the city of Middlesbrough is just to the north of the moors, and the large town of Scarborough on the coast just to the south). Whitby is a handsome town – famous for its associations with Brahm Stoker's novel *Dracula* – with close-packed buildings

Whitby Abbey (Walk 10)

and narrow streets around the boat-filled harbour, all overlooked by the famous ruined abbey *(Walk 10)*. To the north, a sand beach leads to the village of Sandsend, beyond which there are cliffs *(1)*. Behind the village is the dense woodland around Mulgrave Castle *(2)*. The coast south from Whitby to Scarborough is largely of cliffs, and there are some dramatic sections of path along the line of the Cleveland Way *(11,12,13,15)*.

The valley of the River Esk – Eskdale – runs west from Whitby, back into the hills. There is a string of villages along the valley – Sleights, Grosmont, Glaisdale *(5,6)*, Leaholm, Danby *(3)* – linked by a signposted, lineal walk – the Esk Valley Walk – which follows a complex variety of paths, tracks and roads. To the south of the valley is a series of smaller dales carrying tributary becks and rivers, and there are low-level walks through the woodland around the waterfall at Falling Foss *(7)*, and in the valley south of Goathland *(9)*.

To either side of Eskdale are the heather moors which give the area its particular character. There are no true peaks in the district, and the ground never rises above 1500ft/457m, but what the North York Moors does provide is an extensive area of high-level moorland spread over the wide, rounded ridges between the dales. Ridge walks are more common in the west of the area, but there are two fine moorland walks in this guide –

Mulgrave Castle (Walk 2)

on Glaisdale Rigg *(5)* and Fylingdales Moor *(8)*.

South of Eskdale the moors rise to their low watershed then descend gently to the flat farmland around the River Derwent. At the foot of the slope is a line of villages – Ayton, Snainton, Thornton-le-Dale, Pickering *(19)* and others – linked by the A170. The southern slope is unusual in the Moors in that it has been largely given over to conifer woodland. There is a series of fine forestry walks through the extensive Dalby Forest *(17)* – including the path to the dramatic Bridestones (torrs) *(18)* – and further extensive forestry tracks on the routes above Whisperdales *(14)* and in the valley above Pickering. If you prefer more varied woodland, Raincliffe Woods is well worth visiting *(16)*.

The A169 (Pickering to Whitby) crosses the moors in a gap between the forests. Near its high point, at Saltergate, walks head off to east *(20)* and west *(21)*. The latter starts across moorland and returns through Hole of Horcum: a wide natural amphitheatre with provides one of the most popular walking destinations in the Moors.

The Cleveland Way

The map at the start of this section shows the line of the Cleveland Way. As a number of the walks in the guide make use of this path it is worth explaining what it is.

The Cleveland Way is a long distance path, opened in 1969. In total, it runs 110 miles/176km around the moors and along the coast. The western end of the Way is at the village of Helmsley (see the companion guide: *Walks North York Moors: Western Area*). From there it runs west then north-east along the edge of the moors before joining the coast at Saltburn and heading south-east to reach Filey.

The route can be walked in either direction and will take approximately nine days of steady walking to complete. The paths are generally good and the signage clear. In this area the path is entirely coastal and can be joined at numerous points.

The routes in this guide which make use of the Cleveland Way are *Walks 1,10,11,12,13* and *15*.

Cleveland Way Logo

1 Sandsend to Kettleness
B

A stretch of cliff-top coastal path, linking two villages, with a return through farmland. Paths generally clear. Length: **7 miles/11km**; *Total Height Climbed:* **430ft/130m**. *Dramatic coastal scenery.*

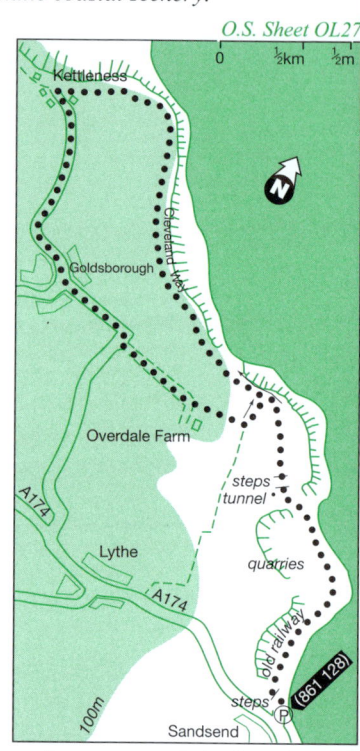

O.S. Sheet OL27

Sandsend is a pretty resort village, 2 miles up the coast from Whitby on the A174. Start from the main car park, at the north end of the village. At the far end of the car park there is a set of steps (sign: Cleveland Way). Climb these and turn right along an old railway line.

Follow this well-maintained path, past old quarry workings and dramatic cliffs, for a mile/1.6km, until it approaches the closed-off entrance to a tunnel. At this point a post indicates the start of a rough path which climbs to the right of the tunnel.

Steps complete the climb. You then cross a headland on a straight path by a field boundary before rejoining the coast. After a short distance a sign points left for a footpath to Lythe. That is your return route; for the moment, continue by the coast.

After a further 2 miles/3.2km, the path reaches Kettleness. Join the public road by the cottages in Kettleness and turn left. After a little under a mile/1.6km the road reaches the crossroads in the middle of the village of Goldsborough. Keep straight on (Lythe). The road runs straight (and narrow: listen out carefully for traffic) for a short distance then turns hard right. Turn first left beyond this (bridleway) on a track heading for Overdale Farm.

As you approach the farm the track splits. Go straight on (yellow arrow). Shortly beyond there is a sign pointing straight on for Sandsend. Walk down the left-hand side of two fields then turn left, by a field boundary, to return to the junction passed before.

2 Mulgrave Woods _____ C

*Clear tracks and paths through fine, mature woodland, leading to a ruined castle. Length: **3¾ miles/6km**; Height Climbed: **260ft/80m**. NB: This walk is on private land. It is closed throughout May and is otherwise open only on Sat., Sun. and Wed.*

O.S. Sheet OL27

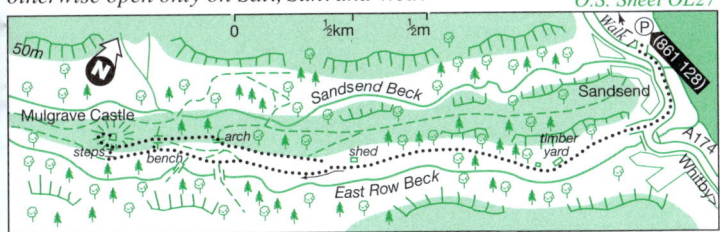

Sandsend is a pretty resort village, 2 miles up the coast from Whitby on the A174. This walk makes use of the numerous paths and tracks through the private woodland around the little valleys to the west (*see* restrictions above). The following is a suggested route to the ruin of Mulgrave Castle (13th-century, with later additions) and back.

Park in the main car park for Sandsend, on the northern edge of the village, then walk south by the road, with the beach down to your left. The road bends inland to cross a bridge over East Row Beck. Turn right immediately before the bridge, into a parking area for a restaurant.

Follow the metalled road from the back of the car park, quickly passing a timber yard and a house and then continuing up the valley. You reach an open, grassy area with a wooden shed at the far end. Just beyond the shed the track splits. Go left.

At the next junction go left again.

Within 50m you pass the end of a stone bridge across the beck. Do not cross this: continue with the beck to your left. After a short distance a track comes in from behind-right. Keep straight on on the clear track, ignoring fainter paths and tracks heading off to the left, until you reach a junction with a bench ahead of you and a tunnel entrance to your right. Keep straight on here.

After a short distance there is a sign pointing right, to the castle. Climb some steps and the slope beyond to reach the castle wall. A diversion to the left will lead to the castle entrance. Afterwards, return to this spot but keep straight on (ie, do not go back down the slope).

The track descends. At its lowest point it forks: go left. At the next junction go right, passing under a stone arch. At a third junction go right again. This will take you back to the wooden shed. From here, return by the original route.

3 Danby Moor

A short moor crossing and a stretch of quiet public road. Fine views.
Length: **4 1/2 miles/7km**; *Total Height Climbed:* **755ft/230m**.

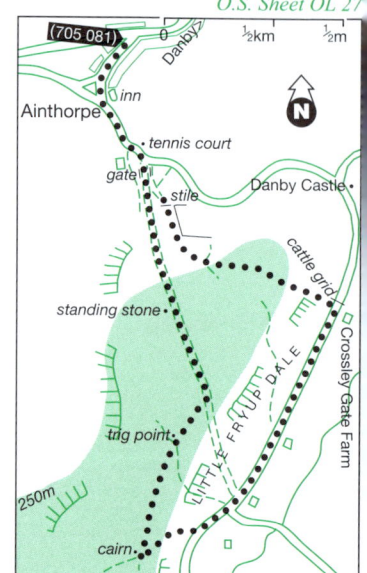

O.S. Sheet OL 27

The little village of Ainthorpe is half a mile south of Danby on a minor road. (Parking is very limited.) From the village, look for the road signed for Fryup and the Fox & Hounds Inn. Follow the road uphill, past the inn and out of the village. You pass a tennis court. Just beyond – just before the highest point of the road – there is a sign to the right for a bridleway.

The clear path starts through gorse and quickly passes through a gate. Beyond this it climbs straight across the open moor, passing a standing stone on the way. Continue until you reach a junction of paths where the main path drops over the edge of the moor to descend into Little Fryup Dale. Turn right here, on the path along the top of the slope (**NB**: this is not a right of way and may be closed for shooting, etc. If this is the case, follow the original path into the dale.)

Follow this path for 1/2 mile/0.8km – passing a trig point, the end of a path coming up from the left, and a line of grouse butts – to reach a four-way junction (collapsed cairn). Turn back-left here and follow a rough path down to the unfenced public road.

Turn left to reach a road junction. Go straight on here and continue down the dale for 3/4 mile/1.2km until you reach Crossley Gate Farm, with a cattle grid ahead. At this point there is a sign pointing left for a footpath.

Climb the steep slope, with a wall to your right. Beyond the top of the slope the path edges away from the wall. Continue across the moor to reach a junction marked by a post with yellow arrows. Keep straight on here, on what appears to be a clear track with a large ditch to the left.

This swings right to join a wall. When you reach a fence, cross a stile. Immediately beyond, join a grassy track which has come in from behind-right. After a short distance you reach a fork. Either path will lead you back to the public road.

4 Great Fryup Dale   B

A short, steep circuit on rough paths, descending into a dale, climbing back out on a dramatic path then returning across moorland. Length: **3½ miles/5.6km**; *Height Climbed:* **625ft/190m**. *Link with Walk 5.*

O.S. Sheet OL 27

The start of this walk can be reached by a number of minor roads from Eskdale. From Leaholm, follow the minor road heading south-west towards Rosedale. After 3½ miles the road swings left (ie, south-east). At this point look for a group of three gates to the right (west) of the road and find room to park on the verge nearby. (Alternatively, the walk can be reached by following Walk 5).

Go through the right-hand (pedestrian) gate. Beyond it, a narrow sheep path runs through the heather. Follow this downhill to a gate in a wall running across the slope above Great Fryup Dale. Go through this and zig-zag down the steep slope below to reach the top of a lane with trees in it. Follow this down to the public road and turn left.

The road passes Fryup Lodge then reaches a gate. Go through this, cross a beck just beyond, then swing left on a clear track, with a field up to your right and the beck to your left.

The track runs through fields to the buildings at Dale Head. Pass to the right of these. Immediately beyond them the track disappears: go right, climbing towards a small fenced area. When you reach this there are two gates. Go through the gate to your right, then climb with the fence to your left to reach a pedestrian gate in a fence running across the slope.

Once through this turn left on a clear path. Follow this, with the fence/wall to your left.

The fence turns away to the left just as you reach a small beck. Cross a footbridge over the beck and continue to a gate in a wall running across the route. Beyond the gate head half-left to ford a beck below a small ruin.

The rough, steep path now climbs the slope at the head of the dale. At the top of the slope the path joins a clear track running along the edge of the moor. Turn left along this to return to the start.

5 Glaisdale Moor_____B

A moderate moorland walk, largely on clear tracks and a quiet public road, but with a trackless section towards the end which can be marshy. Fine views into Glaisdale and Great Fryup Dale. Length: **6½ miles/ 10.4km**; *Height Climbed:* **590ft/180m**. *Possible link with Walk 4.*

O.S. Sheet OL 27

Glaisdale is a small village in Eskdale, about seven miles (by road) west of Sleights. Park and walk to the north end of the village, then turn left up Hall Lane.

Follow the metalled road for ½ mile/0.8km until it ends at a gate. Continue on the clear track beyond, initially with a fence to your left. When the fence turns away to the left the track forks. Keep straight on (ie, the right-hand track) to reach a junction of paths by a small pond.

Just before the pond a bridleway heads back-right and a track heads off to the left. Ignore both of these and follow the clear track to the right of the pond. Just beyond it there is a further junction, with a signposted bridleway heading off to the left. Keep to the right, following the clearer track.

The track continues across moorland, with views into Glaisdale to the left. After ¾ mile/1.2km it passes a small boulder memorial (to the right of the track: Mrs Stainthorpe). Just beyond this a track comes in from behind-left. Ignore this and continue for a short distance to reach a four-way junction.

Keep straight on at the junction (the right-hand track makes a slightly shorter walk – *see* map); climbing for a little over ½ mile/0.8km to join the public road just beyond a trig point.

Turn right down this road (a turn to the left at this point will lead, in ½ mile/0.8km, to a link with Walk 4). There are no walls or fences, and the road runs straight down the top of the ridge, giving fine views. After a short distance you pass a junction with the road into Great Fryup Dale. Ignore this and continue for a further mile/1.6km to reach a four-way road junction.

Turn right here (Glaisdale). The road drops to cross Busco Beck then climbs straight up the far slope. The road swings left. Just before a cattle grid a sign points right for a bridleway. Turn onto a clear track.

The track turns left, into a house. Keep straight on, on a grassy, reedy path. After a short distance this path goes left, through a gate. Keep straight on, with a fence to the left but no clear path.

When the fence cuts away to the left, stop and look ahead. Before you is a heathery, marshy swale, draining to the left and with farms and fields below. There is no clear path across this swale. Looking ahead-left you will see a single walled field, jutting out above the others above the farm at Broad Leas. Choose whichever route you wish through the heather and marsh, but aim for the top edge of that field. Shortly before it you will join a fence. Walk uphill to the right of this fence to return to the gate at the top of Hall Lane.

6 East Arncliff Wood _____ C

A short lineal path through pleasant woodland by the River Esk. Length: **1 mile/1.6km** (one way); *Height Climbed:* **100ft/30m**.

O.S. Sheet OL 27

Drive east from the centre of the village of Glaisdale (*see* Walk 5). After ½ mile you pass the Arncliffe Arms and the road descends to pass beneath a railway bridge. Turn right immediately beyond the bridge into a parking area.

Note the fine 17th-century pack bridge across the river (Beggar's Bridge), then walk in the opposite direction (ie, towards Glaisdale) to reach a footbridge over the Glaisdale Beck.

The path beyond zig-zags up the slope then continues, as a slabbed path, through the wood. Follow this as far as the public road. It is possible to turn left here and follow the road for a mile/1.6km to Egton Bridge, but as the road is walled and narrow it is better to turn back here and return by the same route.

7 Falling Foss _____ B

A complex, low-level circuit through mixed woodland and farmland on tracks and paths of varying quality. The centrepiece is the wooded valley around Falling Foss waterfall. Length: **3½ miles/5.5km***; Total Height Climbed:* **390ft/120m**.

O.S. Sheet OL27

To reach the start of this walk, drive 4 miles south from Whitby on the B1416. A group of three roads heads off to the right (including the road to May Beck – *see* Walk 8). For this walk take the second road, signed for

Falling Foss. Follow this road downhill for ³⁄₄ mile, into a wood. At the point where the road ends and a track begins, there is a car park to the left.

Walk to the car park entrance and turn left, down the track (sign: Falling Foss). After a short distance a rougher path cuts off ahead-right. Follow this down the slope. The waterfall is visible through the trees, with Midge Hall to the left.

Turn right (ie, down the valley) on a clear path with a fence to the left. As you go along, on a ledge on the wooded slope, paths head off to right and left. Ignore these and stick to the main path. You come up through the line of a tumbledown stone wall and there is a signposted junction. Go left here (Littlebeck).

After ¹⁄₄ mile/0.5km you pass The Hermitage – a charming 18th-century folly created by hollowing out a rock to form a cave. Beyond this, the path drops down and across the slope and enters the Little Beck Wood Nature Reserve at the line of an old wall. Follow the clear path for a further ¹⁄₂ mile/1km to reach a gate leading on to the public road as it runs through the little village of Littlebeck.

Turn left along this road, crossing the ford/footbridge. Just beyond this there is a sign for a bridleway to the left. Ignore this. The road swings hard right here but you keep straight on, up a narrow road to the left of a chapel (Intake Farm).

Follow this road steeply uphill, passing houses at first then running straight on to reach Intake Farm.

By the gate into the farm, turn left through a pedestrian gate and walk on along the top of a field, with a fence to your right. Go through two fields this way before rejoining the track and continuing, now with a fence to your left. Follow this track, which runs straight for ¹⁄₂ mile/0.8km, until you reach a signposted four-way junction just before a gate.

Go straight on (bridleway), passing through a gate and heading downhill towards Leas Hill Farm. Just as the track winds left, to reach the buildings, cut off to the right at a bridleway post to go through a gate in the bottom corner of the field.

Beyond this the path heads right, up the valley of a small beck. After a short distance you cross a footbridge over the beck, go through a gate, and continue with a fence to your right and the beck, surrounded by woodland, beyond that.

After 100m the beck bends away to the right and the wood ends. At this point you veer slightly to the left, on a rough path, with gorse to your right and the fence beyond that.

The gorse ends but the rough path continues. Walk up to the top of the field, where there is a wooden gate. Beyond this there is a lane and a signposted junction. Go left (this lane is often very wet and muddy), to reach the empty buildings at Foss Farm. You pass to the right of these. Beyond, paths and tracks head off to the right. Ignore these and follow the clear track, with a fence to the left, back to the start.

8 May Beck to Stony Leas — A

A circuit which starts through commercial forestry on good tracks, then crosses moorland on rough paths and tracks which can be damp in places. Fine views. Length: **7 miles/11km**; Height Climbed: **525ft/160m**.

O.S. Sheet OL27

Stony Leas Boundary Stone

To reach the start of this walk, drive 4 miles south from Whitby on the B1416. A group of three roads heads off to the right (including the road to Falling Foss – *see* Walk 7). For this walk take the third road, signed for May Beck.

At the end of the road – after 1½ miles – the road crosses a bridge over the beck and you turn right into a car park. Walk back to the car park entrance and turn right (ie, as if you had carried straight on after crossing the bridge). You are now on a clear forest road. (This is a cycle route marked by occasional signs; you will be following this route as far as the summit at the southern end of the walk). The track splits immediately, with one heading off to the right and the other straight on. Keep straight on.

The track climbs to a gate then enters a large commercial conifer plantation. After a short way – about half a mile/0.8km from the car park – you reach a junction of tracks. Go left here (sign: cycle route).

The track swings right and reaches another junction. Keep straight on (cycle route). (If you want to be sure you are at the correct junction, if you go a few paces along the track to the right you will see a small, square, concrete reservoir).

The track now swings to the left; passing a small pond then dipping to cross a small stream and climbing to another junction. Go right this time (cycle route). The track now runs clear, twisting to left then right, for a further mile/1.6km before leaving the trees and setting off across the moor.

When the track reaches its highest point there is a gate across it with a pedestrian gate to the right. Go through this. Just beyond there is a junction. Go left here to reach the peak of the hill: marked by a trig point, the mound of Louven Howe (an ancient barrow) and a medieval boundary stone with a cross on it. Looking south from this point there is a fine view, with the truncated pyramid of the radar system at RAF Fylingdales prominent.

Walk on past the summit for a short distance to reach a five-way junction. Go hard left here (arrow). You are now on a clear, rutted, occasionally wet path which runs through moorland for 2½ miles/4km, with the eastern edge of the forest off to the left.

Level with the far end of the forest, the path reaches a signposted four-way junction. Go left here, aiming for a gate in a wall, visible ahead, with a pedestrian gate to the left of it.

Beyond the gate, walk down the edge of the forest to cross a stile leading into a field. There is a small ruin ahead of you. Walk to the left of this and then continue downhill with a broken-down wall to your right.

At the bottom of the field, cross a further stile over a fence and continue downhill across rougher ground (overgrown in places). The path starts by the wall then zig-zags: pulling away to the left then back to the right to reach the road.

Turn left to return to the start.

9 Goathland _____ B

A level walk along an old railway line with a return on rougher paths and tracks above the valley of the Eller Beck. Length: **4½ miles/7km**; *Height Climbed:* undulating.

O.S. Sheet OL 27

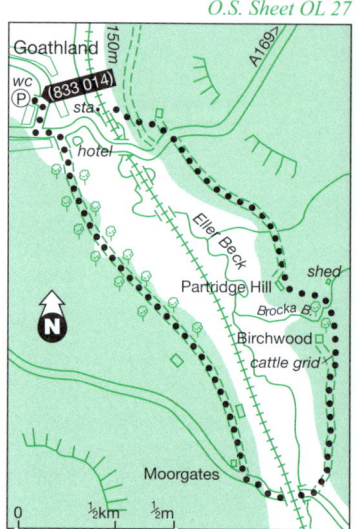

To reach the little village of Goathland, drive two miles south from Sleights on the A169, then turn right onto a minor road for a further two miles. Turn right in the village to reach the car park.

Walk back to the main road through the village and turn left (Whitby). After a short distance turn right, just before the Goathland Hotel, on a track signed as a bridleway. Follow this clear track (on the line of an old railway) through farmland and woodland for a mile/1.6km to reach the public road at Moorgates.

Turn left along the road and follow it under the railway (take great care that there is no traffic when you do this). Follow the road across the Eller Beck and a short way up the slope beyond, then turn left onto a metalled road signed as a bridleway.

The road runs half a mile/0.8km to the buildings at Birchwood. When it runs into the house grounds (cattle grid) keep right, following a grassy path with a wall to your left and the open moor up to the right.

The path descends to reach the stepping stones over Brocka Beck, then continues to the house at Partridge Hill. Pass to the right of the house and join the metalled driveway just beyond. Follow this road across the slope for ¾ mile/1.2km to reach the junction with the public road.

Cross the road and head half-left, towards a house. As you approach the house a sign for a footpath points left. Walk on with a wall to your right. When the wall bends right the path splits, with one going to the right and the other straight on. Go straight on, down and across a slope of grass and bracken to reach a wall at the bottom of the slope.

A clear track runs along the wall. Look for a bench: this marks the point where you turn off this track, following a rough path down and across the slope to reach the railway station on the edge of Goathland.

10 Whitby Coast _____ B

A route from Whitby, past the ruined Abbey and along coastal cliffs, then back through farmland. **Length: 5 miles/8km**; **Height Climbed: 260ft/80m**. *NB: May be unsuitable for small children and animals.*

O.S. Sheet OL27

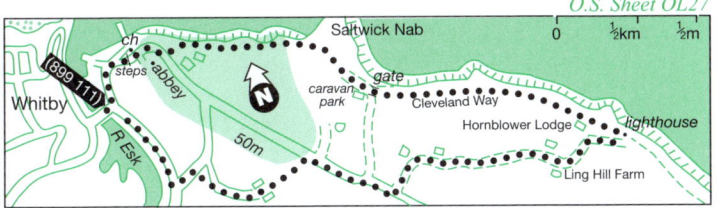

Park in Whitby and walk to the eastern end of the bridge in the town centre (ie, the same side of the river as the Abbey). From the end of the bridge, walk straight up the street ahead for a short distance, then turn left at the sign for Whitby Abbey.

The street swings right and a flight of steps starts to the right. Climb the steps. At the top, go down the right-hand side of St Mary's Church and keep straight on beyond to reach the entrance to the Abbey.

If you are not visiting the Abbey, head left between a wall and a road. The road swings right and, almost immediately, a metalled path heads off to the left, signposted for the Cleveland Way. The path swings right, between buildings and the cliff. At a gate behind the buildings, keep left, outside the fence.

Follow this path by the cliff until it heads inland through a caravan park. Follow the road past the park buildings. When it swings right, just beyond, there is a gate in the fence to your left (Cleveland Way).

Go through this and walk along the bottom of a field, with a fence to your left and the cliffs beyond that.

Continue along the coast for a mile/1.6km; passing the old fog signal station (Hornblower Lodge) then walking on towards the lighthouse. On the near side of the lighthouse the path climbs to join the entrance road. Turn right on this.

The entrance road climbs to Ling Hill Farm and turns right. At the next farm it goes left, up to the road. Turn right here (the road can be busy but there is a path to the left for most of the way). Pass two entrances to the right of the road then watch for a sign (footpath) pointing left. Walk down the left-hand edge of a field, aiming for some buildings. Pass straight through the buildings, now on a metalled entrance road.

The road approaches some houses and turns hard right. Keep straight on here, on a clear path; dropping to join a road (Green Lane). Turn left down this, then right at a T-junction to return to the centre of Whitby.

Walks North York Moors: East

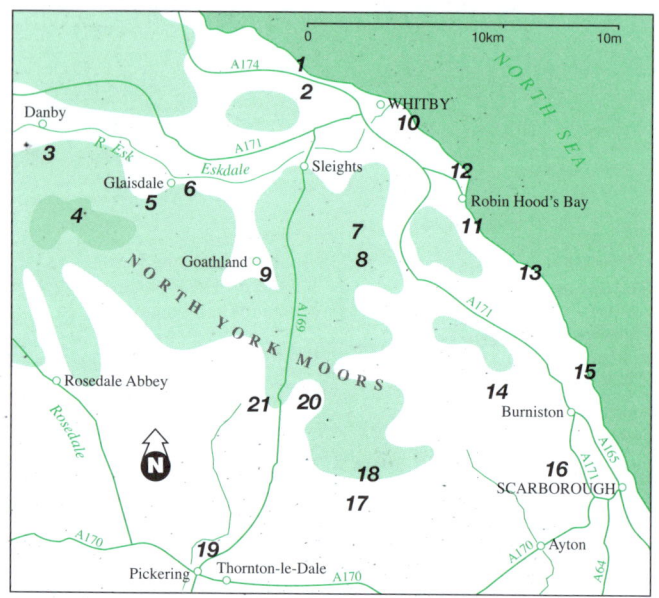

Grades

A ...... Full walking equipment required

B ...... Strong walking footwear and waterproof clothing required

C ...... Comfortable walking footwear recommended

NB: Assume each walk increases at least one grade in winter conditions. Hill routes can become treacherous.

Walks North York Moors: East

walk	grade
1 Sandsend to Kettleness	B
2 Mulgrave Woods	C
3 Danby Moor	B
4 Great Fryup Dale	B
5 Glaisdale Moor	B
6 East Arncliff Wood	C
7 Falling Foss	B
8 May Beck to Stony Leas	A
9 Goathland	B
10 Whitby Coast	B
11 Robin Hood's Bay to Ravenscar	A
12 Robin Hood's Bay & Ness Point	B
13 Ravenscar	B
14 Whisperdales	B
15 Cloughton to Hayburn Wyke	B
16 Raincliffe Woods	C
17 Dalby Forest Walks	B/C
18 Bridestones	B
19 Pickering	B
20 Crosscliff Wood & Blakey Topping	A
21 Hole of Horcum	B

— www.pocketwalks.com —

Published by: *Hallewell Publications, Scotland*
Printed by: *Barr Printers, Glenrothes*

While every care has been taken in the preparation of this guide, the publishers cannot accept responsibility for any loss, damage or injury resulting from its use.

11 Robin Hood's Bay to Ravenscar⎯⎯⎯⎯⎯A

*A flat path through farmland and woodland, with a return along the coastal cliffs. Possible link with Walk 13. **Length: 9 miles/14.5km;** Height Climbed: **490ft/150m** (undulations throughout). **NB:** Cliff-top walking; may be unsuitable for small children and animals.*

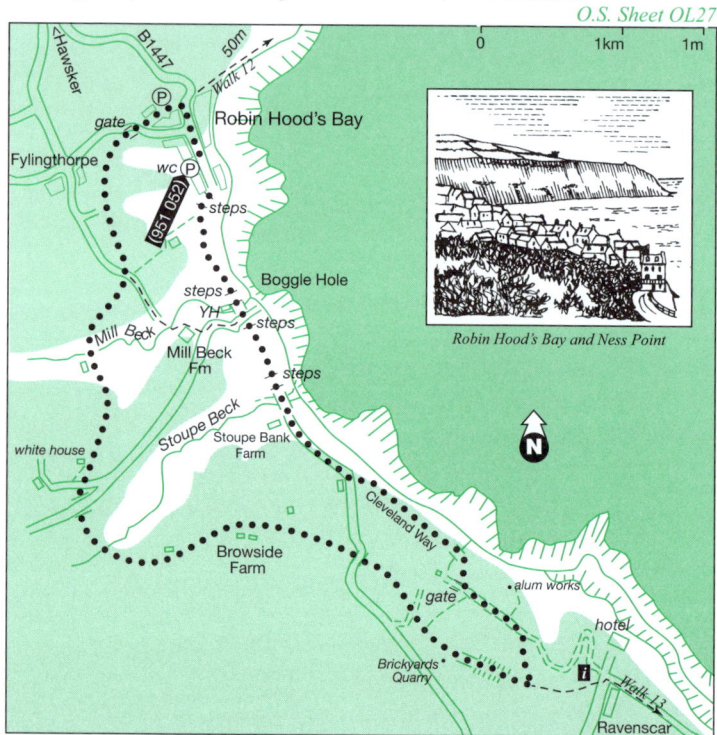

Robin Hood's Bay and Ness Point

O.S. Sheet OL27

There are two car parks in the village of Robin Hood's Bay (*see* map). If you have parked in the one at the foot of the 'new' village, walk back up through the village, keeping straight on at the junction (Hawsker, B1447).

When the road turns right (to pass through the old railway line) go left, into the upper car park. Walk down the left-hand side of the car park. At the far end, keep to the left of the old station buildings and follow the metalled track beyond down to a junction with a road.

Cross the road (carefully) and follow it to the right for a short distance to reach a field gate and pedestrian gate to your left. Go through this and you are on the old railway line (signposted as 'Cinder Track').

After half a mile/0.8km you cross a road. A turn to the left here (Boggle Hole) provides a shortened version of this route (*see* map). For the longer walk, keep straight on.

After a further mile/1.6km the track runs to the left of a white house. Just beyond this the track splits. Keep left here; dropping to cross a small road then climbing the far bank and continuing along the old railway.

Continue along the railway. After a further 2½ miles/4km you reach the entrance to the disused Brickyards Alum Quarry to the right of the track (National Trust). Continue along the old railway.

You reach a signposted junction. At this point you have a choice. If you keep straight on you will reach the National Trust Ravenscar Visitor Centre, with its shop and café, and a possible link with Walk 13. Otherwise, cut back to the left (Cleveland Way).

The path joins a very clear track, coming in from behind-right. Go ahead-left along this. After a short distance there is a signposted diversion to the right to visit the ruins of the old (1650-1860) alum works. (Alum is a chemical compound which acts as a fixative for dyes.)

Having visited the ruins, continue along the track for a short way to reach a gate and a signposted junction.

Head off to the right here (Cleveland Way). You are now on a rough footpath, heading towards the sea. The path swings left, over a footbridge over a stream, then continues along the cliff top.

Follow this path for a mile/1.6km until it turns left and joins a metalled road. Turn right along this road, which ends at Stoupe Bank Farm. Continue beyond on a flight of steps, descending to cross a concrete footbridge over Stoupe Beck.

At the far end of the bridge the path splits: one goes right (to the beach) and one goes left. But for this route go straight on, climbing a flight of steps then continuing along the cliff.

After half a mile/0.8km a further set of steps leads down to the metalled road to the slipway at Boggle Hole. Turn right down the road, for a short distance, then first left on a clear path leading up to the footbridge over Mill Beck, just below the Youth Hostel.

At the far end of the bridge the entrance to the Youth Hostel is to your left (tearoom), but for this route keep straight on; climbing stone steps to continue along the cliffs.

You reach a T-junction with another path. Go right here and continue to the long flight of steps leading down to the old section of Robin Hood's Bay. Walk up through the village to return to the start.

12 Robin Hood's Bay & Ness Point _____ B

A short path along the cliff-tops north of Robin Hood's Bay with a return by the old railway line. Length: **4 miles/6.5km**; Height Climbed: **200ft/60m**. *NB: Cliff-top walking; may be unsuitable for small children and animals.*

O.S. Sheet OL27

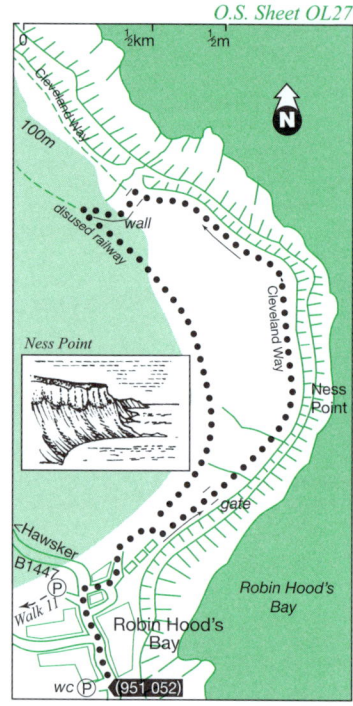

There are two car parks in the village of Robin Hood's Bay (*see map*). If you have parked in the one at the foot of the 'new' village, it is only a short detour down the slope beyond to visit the picturesque old village (*see also* Walk 11). For this route, however, walk back up through the village, keeping straight on at the junction (Hawsker, B1447).

After a short distance the road goes hard right (the entrance to the upper car park is to the left at this point), then left (through a gap in the old railway). Turn off to the right before the railway, on Mount Pleasant North.

At the end of a row of houses, follow the signs for the Cleveland Way, left then right on a clear track. After a short distance, turn right at a sign for the Cleveland Way, off the main track. Climb to a gate. Go through this, crossing the Rocket Post Field, to reach a further gate. Go through this and turn left.

Follow the path through a gate. Beyond this you continue along the edge of a field, with a fence and cliff-top to the right. After crossing a small stream, the fence moves to the left and you now have the open cliff to your right – take care.

Follow the path around the point and continue until you see a large black cliff ahead of you. As the path begins to climb to reach the top of this cliff, head off to the left through a kissing gate (to railway path). The path climbs with a wall to the left, between two small valleys, to join the line of the old railway.

Turn left along the old railway line to return to the village.

13 Ravenscar — B

A path along a section of old railway line and a return along the cliff tops. Muddy in places. Length: **5 miles/8km**; *Height Climbed:* **165ft/50m**. *Possible link with Walk 11.*

Ravenscar is a tiny, scattered village, including buildings which were intended to be the heart of a coastal resort which was never built. To reach it, drive six miles north from Scarborough on the A171 and turn right. There is parking to the left of the road, just before you reach the National Trust Coastal Centre and Raven Hall Hotel.

Walk on along the road, turning hard right at the hotel entrance and continuing for half a mile/0.8km to reach the buildings around a little square. Turn right here, through the square, to reach the old railway line. Turn left along this.

Follow the line for 1½ miles/2.5km, through farmland, until it descends into a wooded area around a stream. Watch for a stile to the left, by a stretch of wooden fence. Cross this stile and go down some steps to reach another. Beyond this the path splits: one going right and the other straight on. Go straight on.

The path is rough and wet here, but there is little doubt about the route. Climb to a group of gates. Jink to the left then go through a gate which allows you to continue in the same direction. Keep straight on to reach a gate leading on to a metalled track. Turn left along this.

The track runs straight for a short distance then turns half-left. At this

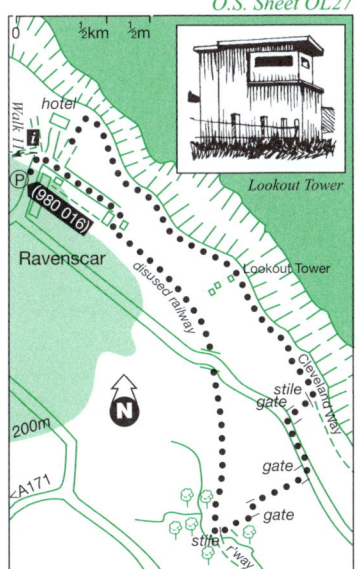

point you will see two gates to your right. Go through the right-hand gate and walk down the edge of a field with a wall to your left.

Cross a stile at the bottom corner of the field and turn left along the cliff-top path (Cleveland Way). The clear path passes the old coastguard lookout tower (with a wartime radar station behind it) then continues along the coast until it reaches the edge of the hotel grounds. Turn left here to return to the road.

14 Whisperdales _____B

A circuit, largely on clear, rough paths and tracks, through commercial forestry and farmland. Fine views. Length: **5½ miles/9km**; *Height Climbed:* **430ft/130m**.

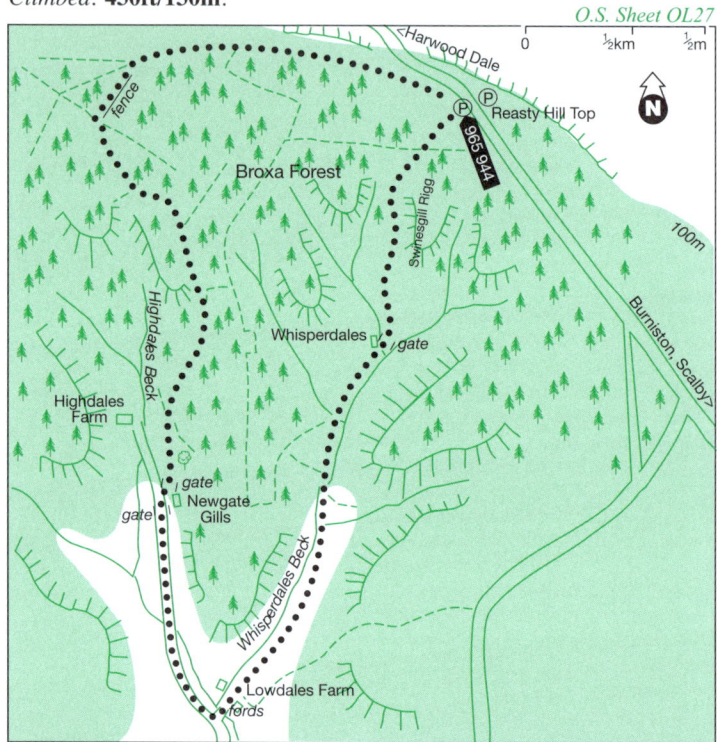

Reasty Hill Top (the site of the car park at the start of this walk) is part of the ridge – steep on the north-east face; gentle to the south-west – which runs north-west from Scarborough. To reach it, drive north from Scarborough on the A171 for about 2 miles to reach the village of Burniston. At the northern end of the village, turn left (west) onto a minor road signposted for Hackness. After a short distance, turn left again (Hackness). Follow this road out of the village and on for 1½ miles to a T-junction. Turn right here (Harwood Dale) and drive on for 2 miles to the point just before the road drops over the edge of the ridge. At this point there are car parks to either side of the road.

Start walking from the car park to the left (south-west) of the road. Walk to the far (north) end of the car park and join a forest track. A signpost points to bridleways to the right (ie, along the ridge) and ahead (ie, into the forest). Go straight ahead, into the forest.

After a short distance a path comes in from behind-left and heads off ahead-right. Ignore this and keep straight on, following the clear, main track which runs straight for a while then swings to the left and drops down and across the wooded slope of Swinesgill Rigg.

The track leaves the trees and continues through fields to pass to the left of the house at Whisperdales. Just before the house is a gate, marked by a blue arrow. Go through this and continue – now with only a rough path – along the bottom of a field with Whisperdales Beck to your left.

The path runs through a number of fields, gradually becoming clearer and always running near the beck. Approximately level with the end of a wooded hill to your left, the main track bends left to run up a side valley. Ignore this and continue as before, now on a fainter path.

The path runs down to the buildings around Lowdales Farm. Cross the footbridges by the fords to reach the public road. (Two becks join here and often overflow their banks; a post beside the ford show the water depth.) Turn right, up the road.

Walk up the narrow public road (a sunken lane in places, so be careful of any traffic) to the house at Newgate Gills. Go through a gate just before it and follow a clear track below and to the left of the building. Just beyond the house there is a gate with a pedestrian gate to the right of it. Go through the pedestrian gate (bridleway) and follow the clear path through woodland.

A conifer plantation starts to the right and a track crosses from behind-right to ahead-left. Cross this and continue climbing on a clear path (arrow).

At the end of the straight climb you reach a clear, unsignposted fork in the path. Go left.

Follow this very clear path, ignoring smaller paths to right and left. After a short distance, views open up through the trees over the valley of the Highdales Beck, down to your left.

After you leave the head of the valley, the path runs straight to reach a junction with a clear track, crossing from behind-right to ahead-left. Walk a few paces to the left along this track, then turn off it to the right, following a clear path with a fence to your right.

This path runs straight to join the clear track along the edge of the ridge. Turn right on this and follow it along the ridge for a mile/1.6km to return to the start.

15 Cloughton to Hayburn Wyke _____ B

A moderate circuit, along a wooded cliff top to a rocky beach then back by the old railway line. Length: **4$\frac{1}{2}$ miles/7km**; *Total Height Climbed:* **460ft/140m**. *NB: Cliff-top walking; may be unsuitable for small children and animals.*

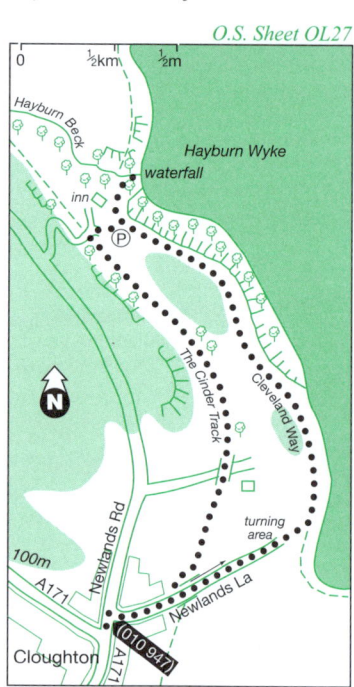

O.S. Sheet OL27

The little village of Cloughton is about 3 miles north of Scarborough on the A171. Parking is limited.

At the north end of the village there is a junction. Turn onto Newlands Road then turn right, immediately, down Newlands Lane. Keep straight on down this road; out of the village, over the old railway line (the return route) and down to the turning area behind the coast.

Follow the path from here in the direction of the sea. This joins the clear coastal path (Cleveland Way). Turn left. The path starts quite low, then climbs to run along the top of a wooded cliff, sometimes between hedges. There are fine views.

The path eventually enters the woodland around Hayburn Wyke (National Trust) and starts to descend into a small valley. Keep following the signs for the Cleveland Way. As you approach Hayburn Beck there is a T-junction. To complete the circuit you will be going left, but first go right, down steps, for a short distance, to look at the rocky beach, cliffs and little waterfall at Hayburn Wyke.

Return to the junction and go straight on along a clear path. Go through a gate at the edge of the trees, then go half-right to reach a further gate (arrow). Go through this. You are now on a clear metalled track.

After a short distance a path cuts left, leading to a car park. To visit the inn, keep straight on here. To complete the route, go left, through the car park. Go out the entrance to the car park and the old railway (Cinder Track) starts immediately to your left. Turn left here and follow the clear path back to Newlands Lane.

16 Raincliffe Woods _____ C

An extensive area of fine mixed broad-leaved and conifer woodland to the west of Scarborough. Three waymarked walks have been laid out through the woods. Generally clear paths and some fine views, but all three routes contain steep sections. Lengths: **1½-3¾ miles/2.4-6km**; *Height Climbed:* up to **430ft/130m**.

O.S. Sheet OL 27

Raincliffe Woods lie directly to the west of Scarborough, on a north/north-west facing escarpment overlooking a valley. To reach them, drive along the A171, through the western edge of the town, and watch for a sign. This points you onto a minor road which runs west along the foot of the slope on its way to West Ayton.

There are nine car parks for the woods (*see* map); the most easterly by little Throxenby Mere and the most westerly on the road up through Forge Valley.

The narrow band of woodland reaches from the road to the edge of the level farmland above the slope and is two miles/3.2km in length. There are numerous connected paths and tracks through the woods, so it is possible to follow the well-signposted waymarked walks, link them together, or make up your own route.

The waymarked walks have been laid out by the Friends of Raincliffe Woods, and coloured maps can be seen at each of the car parks. All of the walks include some climbing. The shortest (green) route climbs only 130ft/40m, but if you have the time and energy it is worth taking on one of the other two routes, which climb to the top of the wooded bank.

17 Dalby Forest Walks — B/C

A selection of waymarked forest walks from different start points. A leaflet is available from the Dalby Visitor Centre. Lengths: see map. *See also Walk 18.*

O.S. Sheet OL27

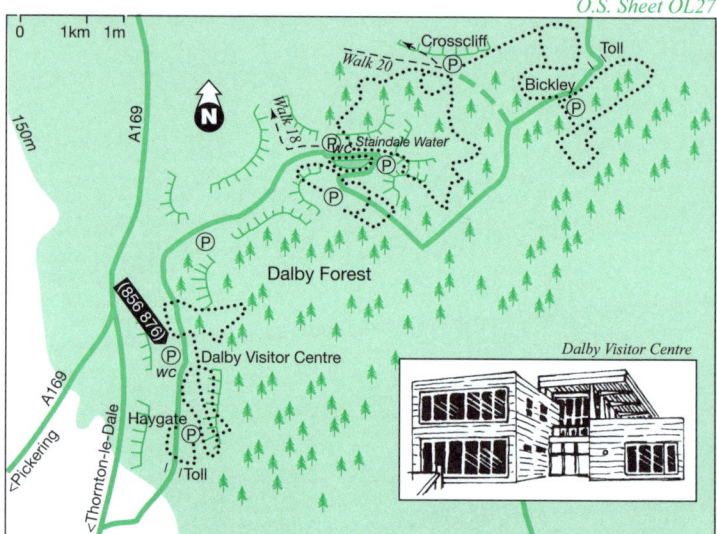

Dalby is a large commercial forest in the south-east of the North York Moors area. It is well laid out for walkers and cyclists, with a toll road (fee) providing access to a visitor centre, shops, a restaurant and a number of car parks. The most famous walk in the area is to the Bridestones (*see* Walk 18), but the straightforward forest walks are well laid out and signposted.

The toll road has two entrances, but the southern one is the easier to find. Drive 2 miles east from the centre of Pickering on the A170 to reach the crossroads in the centre of the village of Thornton-le-Dale. Turn left (north) here and follow the road for a little over a mile to reach a junction with a minor road which turns off to the right. The toll is a short way along this road and the visitor centre and main car park are about 1½ miles further on.

There are 13 waymarked walks in total, starting from seven different car parks. The routes and car parks are shown on the map. For more information, a leaflet is available from the visitor centre.

18 Bridestones
B

A short loop on rough paths, climbing through woodland to a line of spectacular natural sculpted boulders. Length: **2 miles/3km**; *Height Climbed:* **260ft/80m**.

O.S. Sheet OL27

This well-known walk starts from the Low Staindale car park in Dalby Forest (*see* Walk 17 for driving instructions; please note that a fee is due for driving the toll road). Low Staindale is to the left of the road, a little over 2½ miles after the visitor centre. If you pass Staindale Water, you have gone just too far.

Follow the path out of the car park. After a short distance you pass a sign – National Trust: Bridestones – and a map of the route. Just beyond you reach a kissing-gate leading into a field. Go through this and follow the grassy path along the top of the field, parallel to the fence to the right.

You approach a small stream. The main path drops to cross the stream, but before you reach it a fainter path heads off half-right. This is the path to the Bridestones.

Go through a kissing-gate then cross the beck on a wooden footbridge. Continue by the beck, recrossing it at the next footbridge, then climb up out of the valley. A well-made path leads up onto the ridge of Needle Point.

When the path reaches the first of the rocks it turns hard right. A short diversion at this point, straight ahead, will lead along the foot of a row of such rocks. After looking at these, return to the first rock and continue along the path: dropping to cross a beck then climbing to the top of the far slope.

A path comes in from the left. Ignore this and walk down the ridge of heather and bracken, passing the most dramatic of the Bridestones. Just beyond the last rock a path heads off to the left. Ignore this and keep straight on. The clear path swings left, drops into a larch wood and returns to the junction by the first gate.

19 Pickering

A woodland walk up the valley of Pickering Beck, starting past the old castle then continuing along paths of varying quality and a stretch of public road. Length: **5½ miles/8.8km**; *Height Climbed:* undulating.

O.S. Sheet OL 27

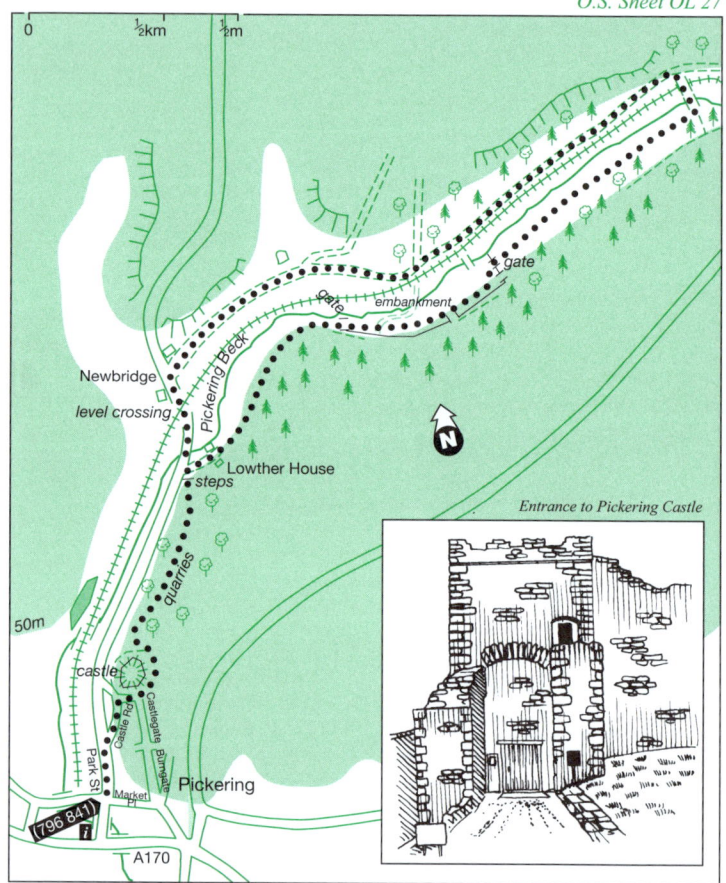

Entrance to Pickering Castle

Park in the town of Pickering and walk north, following the signs for the ruined Norman castle on the edge of the village. The castle is worth visiting on its own account, but for this walk turn right from the castle entrance on the Pickering Castle Path. This goes round the outside of the castle, starting in the dry bed of the moat.

When you reach the far side of the castle a path cuts off to the right, leading into the woods. Turn on to this. At the first split keep left, heading downhill. From this point there are numerous paths and junctions. For this walk, just make sure that you are running near the edge of the wood and parallel to the road, down to your left. You will pass a number of old quarries along the way.

The path joins the road by dropping down some steps to a small turning place. There is a sign for Lowther House and a metalled driveway heading off to your right. Follow this driveway towards a house, with a wooded bank to your right.

Go through a pedestrian gate by the house, then walk on between it and its garages to reach a second gate. Go through this and continue along a clear footpath at the bottom of a wooded slope, with Pickering Beck to your left.

The beck pulls away but the path (damp in places) continues along the bottom of the wood, with a fence to the left.

You reach a pedestrian gate. Go through this and you are in a long, narrow, curving field (grazing livestock; take care). Walk along the top of this, climbing over the end of a large concrete flood embankment then continuing, with the trees to your right.

Ignore gates through the fence to your right and continue, to reach a gate in the far left-hand corner of the field, just by the beck, leading into a wood. (Interpretive panel.) Beyond this, a clear path (damp in places) leads through the trees.

After $^1/_2$ mile/0.8km you reach a junction with another path. Go left, crossing a wooden footbridge over the beck then climbing to a gate leading onto the railway line. Cross the line (carefully), go through the gate on the far side and climb a short flight of steps to join a clear track. Turn left along this.

Follow this track by the railway for $^1/_2$ mile/0.8km (if you are lucky you may see one of the steam trains which regularly run along this line) to join a clearer track. Turn left along this and follow it for a further $^3/_4$ mile/1.2km. It becomes a metalled road after a while, before ending at a junction with a larger road at Newbridge.

Turn left along this road, crossing a level crossing then continuing. After a short distance you will see the Lowther House driveway to the left. At this point, either return by your original route (through the wood and back by the castle) or just continue on the pavement to the right of the road, back into Pickering.

20 Crosscliff Wood & Blakey Topping _____ A

This circuit starts as a level path, through farmland at first and then forestry, along the top of a ridge, then returns via farmland, moorland and a short climb up an isolated hill. Paths clear throughout. Length: **8 miles/13km**; *Total Height Climbed:* **720ft/220m**.

O.S. Sheet OL27

Blakey Topping from the south

This walk starts from the Saltergate car park, 6 miles north of the town of Pickering on the A169 (also the starting point for Walk 21). Walk to the north end of the car park then on a little further up the right-hand side of the road to reach a junction with a clear track, cutting off to the right, signed for Crosscliff. Follow this metalled track through a narrow band of conifers.

On the far edge of the trees a sign points left for a bridleway. Ignore this and keep straight on; passing through a pedestrian gate and continuing along the clear track. After ³/₄ mile/1.2km you reach a junction by some sheep pens. A concrete track heads down to the left. This is the return route, but for now keep straight on along a rougher track along the top of the slope.

The track enters an area of woodland. There are occasional paths heading off to right and left beyond this, but ignore these and continue along Crosscliff Brow. After about 1¹/₂ miles/2.5km the main track heads right, into the forest. Keep straight on, along a cinder path, to reach a viewpoint. Immediately beyond this there is a junction. Go back-left here (no sign), following a clear track down and across the slope.

Go through a gate at the bottom of the wood and continue. After 100m you reach a junction with a track heading off to the left. Turn onto this track and follow it for ¹/₂ mile/0.8km to a ford over little Crosscliff Beck. Cross this and follow the track beyond to the left of a farmhouse. Just beyond this you reach a gate leading onto the moorland of Thompson's Rigg.

You are now on a rough, clear vehicle track. After a short distance a signposted footpath heads off to the left. Ignore this and continue.

On the far side of the moor, with the sharp peak of Blakey Topping visible ahead, you reach a gate/stile. Cross this and continue, initially with a fence to the left, climbing through grassland. The track swings to the left and passes through another gate, with a group of standing stones just beyond. Turn right beyond this gate and walk on with a fence to your right.

You reach the top corner of the field, with the corner of a conifer wood ahead and a gate to the right. To make a diversion up Blakey Topping from this point go right, through the gate. Climb with a fence to your left for 40m then turn left, across a stile, and continue climbing up a straight, steep path to the top of the hill.

Return to the corner of the field and walk downhill, with the edge of the forest to your right. Pass through a gate at the lowest point of the path then climb up to Newgate Foot farm. The track passes through the farm buildings – with the house to your left – then swings right, up and across the slope, to return to the junction at the top of the brow.

Turn right and retrace your steps to return to the start.

21 Hole of Horcum _____ B

A moderate circuit, starting across open moorland and returning through grazing land in a pleasant valley. Paths generally clear.
Length: **5 miles/8km**; *Height Climbed:* **490ft/150m**.

O.S. Sheet OL27

This walk starts from the Saltergate car park, 6 miles north of Pickering on the A169 (also the starting point for Walk 20).

Cross the road (carefully) and turn right, following the path running parallel to the road and overlooking the great natural hollow of Hole of Horcum. When the road bends away hard right keep straight on, following the clear path to a gate/stile (the path coming in from the left before the gate is you return route).

Cross the stile and continue along this clear path for 2 miles/3km; running level as far as little Seavy Pond (avoid the path heading off to the right here) then descending to the low point of the path at Dundale Pond.

Here there is a signposted junction. Turn left (sign: Dundale Griff) and follow a rough, clear path down the right-hand side of a deep, wooded gully. The gully ends and the path continues down a short valley to a junction with a larger valley. Here there is a signposted junction. Go left (Hole of Horcum).

A wooden footbridge crosses the beck. Cross this and turn left, with a wall to your right and the beck to your left. You go through a gate and the wall pulls away to the right. Continue with a fence to your left.

Pass through another gate and you are in a sloping field with a wood up to your right. Follow the clear, grassy path across the middle of the fields as far as the ruin of Low Horcum farmstead.

Pass to the left of the ruin and continue in the same direction, with a field boundary to the right, to reach a point where the path crosses the beck. Follow the clear path beyond; climbing up and across the slope to return to the A169.